CULTURE IN ACTION

Roald Dahl

Jane Bingham

Chicago, Illinois

www.heinemannraintree.com
Visit our website to find out more information about Heinemann-Raintree books.

To order:
☎ Phone 888-454-2279
💻 Visit www.heinemannraintree.com to browse our catalog and order online.

©2010 Raintree
an imprint of Capstone Global Library, LLC
Chicago, Illinois

Edited by Louise Galpine and Rachel Howells
Designed by Kimberly Miracle and Betsy Wernert
Original illustrations © Capstone Global Library Ltd.
Illustrated by kja-artists.com
Picture research by Mica Brancic and Kay Altwegg
Production by Alison Parsons
Originated by Steve Walker, Capstone Global Library Ltd
Printed in China by Leo Paper Products Ltd

13 12 11 10 09
10 9 8 7 6 5 4 3 2 1

Library of Congress Cataloging-in-Publication Data
Bingham, Jane.
  Roald Dahl / Jane Bingham.
    p. cm. -- (Culture in action)
  Includes bibliographical references and index.
  ISBN 978-1-4109-3405-5 -- ISBN 978-1-4109-3422-2 (pbk.)
  1. Dahl, Roald--Juvenile literature. 2. Authors, English--20th century--Biography--Juvenile literature. 3. Children's stories--Authorship--Juvenile literature. I. Title.
  PR6054.A35Z417 2009
  823'.914--dc22
  [B]
                              2008054327

Acknowledgments
The author and publishers are grateful to the following for permission to reproduce copyright material: A P Watt Ltd on behalf of Quentin Blake p. **10**; Alamy pp. **12** (Graham Bell), **26** (Clive Thompson People); Corbis pp. **19 top** (Skyscan), **19 bottom** (Tony Savino); Getty Images pp. **6** (Popperfoto), **13** (Popperfoto), **27** (MJ Kim); iStockphoto p. **8** (© Markus Divis); Mary Evans Picture Library p. **9 left**; Quentin Blake p. **18** (Reprinted by permission of The Random House Group Ltd); Reprinted by permission of The Random House Group Ltd pp. **5, 9 right**; Rex Features pp. **4** (ITV), **20, 21** (Jonathan Hordle); Roald Dahl Museum pp. **7** (Dahl & Dahl), **15** (Dahl & Dahl), **22** (Dahl & Dahl), **24** (Dahl & Dahl); The Kobal Collection pp. **5** (Warner Bros./Peter Mountain), **14** (Tri Star), **16** (Warner Bros./Peter Mountain), **23** (UA/EON/Danjaq).

Icon and banner images supplied by Shutterstock: © Alexander Lukin, © ornitopter, © Colorlife, and © David S. Rose.

Cover photograph of Roald Dahl, reproduced with permission of Rex Features (ITV).

We would like to thank Jackie Murphy and Nancy Harris for their invaluable help in the preparation of this book.

Every effort has been made to contact copyright holders of material reproduced in this book. Any omissions will be rectified in subsequent printings if notice is given to the publisher.

All the Internet addresses (URLs) given in this book were valid at the time of going to press. However, due to the dynamic nature of the Internet, some addresses may have changed, or sites may have changed or ceased to exist since publication. While the author and publisher regret any inconvenience this may cause readers, no responsibility for any such changes can be accepted by either the author or the publisher.

Contents

Who Was Roald Dahl?. 4

Early Childhood 6

School Days. 12

Adult Adventures 18

A Lifetime of Writing 22

A Very Special Writer 26

Timeline *28*

Glossary *30*

Find Out More. *31*

Index *32*

Some words are printed in bold, **like this**. You can find out what they mean by looking in the glossary on page 30.

Who Was Roald Dahl?

Roald Dahl is one of the world's most popular children's writers. He is famous for writing amazing storybooks, such as *Charlie and the Chocolate Factory* and *Danny the Champion of the World*. He also wrote some funny poems and two books about his early life.

Great ideas

Roald Dahl lived until he was 74. During his life, he had many adventures. He had some happy times, but some sad things happened to him, too. Dahl met some extremely strange people. These experiences gave him great ideas for his stories.

What's your favorite?

Altogether, there are more than 20 books by Roald Dahl for children. These are just a few of his best-known stories. Is your favorite book on this list?

- *Charlie and the Chocolate Factory*
- *James and the Giant Peach*
- *Danny the Champion of the World*
- *The BFG*
- *Matilda*

Roald Dahl had a fantastic imagination. He wrote children's books for almost 30 years.

This is a scene from the 2005 movie *Charlie and the Chocolate Factory*.

Amazing books

Roald Dahl's books take you on wild adventures. They have fantastic characters, like the Big Friendly Giant (BFG) and Willy Wonka, who has an amazing chocolate factory. They also contain some surprising words, such as "Muggle-Wump" and "scrumdiddlyumptious." Roald Dahl's books can be scary, disgusting, and funny. They tell unforgettable stories.

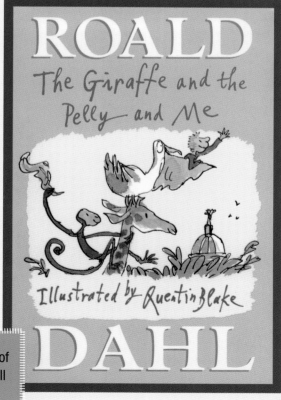

The Giraffe and the Pelly and Me is one of Roald Dahl's shortest stories, but it is still crammed full of action and surprises.

Early Childhood

Roald Dahl never forgot his childhood. Even when he was very old, he said that he could still remember exactly how it felt to be a child. Most of his books are told from a child's point of view. In *Danny the Champion of the World*, Danny tells the story of what happens to him and his father. In *George's Marvellous Medicine* you see the adults from George's viewpoint.

Writing it down

When Roald was in his sixties, he wrote a book for children called *Boy: Tales of Childhood*. It is full of stories about his life from before he left school.

A hero's name

Roald was named after the famous Norwegian explorer, Roald Amundsen. In 1911 Amundsen was the first person to reach the South Pole. No wonder Roald Dahl grew up dreaming of adventures! This photograph shows Amundsen beside the Norwegian flag that he planted at the South Pole.

This photograph shows Roald with his three sisters, Alfhilde, Else, and Asta.

A family from Norway

Roald's parents both came from Norway, but his family lived in Wales. At home the family spoke Norwegian. Altogether, there were six children—one boy and three girls, plus an older stepsister and stepbrother from his father's first marriage.

The Dahl family lived in a large, comfortable house, but Roald's childhood was not always happy. When he was three years old, his stepsister died from **appendicitis**. Later that year, his father died. Roald became very close to his mother.

When he was young, Roald imagined that the Norwegian country was full of giants and witches.

Trips to Norway

After Roald's father died, the family took a vacation in Norway every summer. They would stay with their grandparents part of the time. Then they would sail to an island where they had a great time swimming, fishing, and sailing.

Witches and giants

Roald loved the wild Norwegian country. He also liked the scary stories about witches and giants that his grandmother told him. Later, he included giants and witches in some of his stories.

Norwegian fairy tales often include witches and magical animals. This is the witch Hennegraben and her magical hen.

A wonderful grandmother

In *The Witches*, the hero (who is never named) has a Norwegian grandmother. She is kind, funny, and great at telling stories. This character was based on a mixture of Roald Dahl's mother and grandmother.

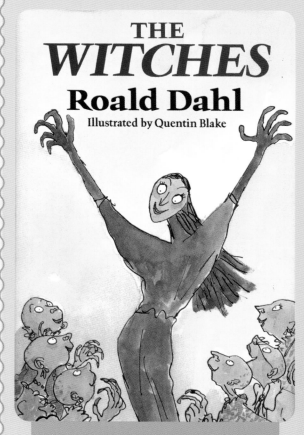

THE
WITCHES
Roald Dahl
Illustrated by Quentin Blake

The story *The Witches* was probably influenced by the fairy tales that Roald's grandmother told him.

Cut it out!

A horrible thing happened to Roald when he was in Norway. He had very swollen adenoids (fleshy lumps between the back of the nose and throat), so his mother took him to a doctor. The doctor cut out the adenoids with a knife!

Roald described this gory experience in vivid detail in *Boy: Tales of Childhood*. He often put gruesome scenes in his books. For example, at the end of *The Twits*, Mr. and Mrs. Twit get stuck doing headstands until their bodies squash into their heads.

In this picture Sophie and the BFG are creeping up on nasty giants.

The BFG

The BFG is one of Roald Dahl's most popular books. It tells the story of Sophie, who becomes friends with a Big Friendly Giant (the BFG). Together they fight some very nasty giants, with names such as Bonecruncher, Gizzardgulper, and Childchewer.

Different characters

As you read *The BFG*, you get to know the different characters. Sophie is sometimes scared, but she is always curious and determined. The BFG is gentle and kind. He has his own wonderful way of speaking, using words such as "swizzfiggling" and "gobblefunking." The nasty giants are fierce, noisy, and violent.

Music for giants

Why not try to create music and dance for Sophie, the BFG, and the nasty giants? You can work on your own, in pairs, or in a group.

Steps to follow:

1. What kind of tune expresses Sophie's character? How can you portray the BFG and his strange way of talking? What sounds could you use for the nasty giants? You can clap rhythms and use your voice, or you can use musical instruments, such as a recorder and drums.

2. When you have made up your tunes, try creating dances for the different characters. You could make small, delicate movements for Sophie, and take huge strides for the BFG. The nasty giants could make heavy thumping steps, and punch their fists in the air. Use your imagination to think of other examples!

3. Read the chapter where Sophie and the BFG use the dream trumpet to frighten the nasty giants. Then try telling the story using your own music and dance.

School Days

When Roald was seven years old, he went to a school for boys. Every day when he walked to school with his friends, he passed a store window filled with candy. It was the beginning of his lifelong interest in chocolate and candy.

Nasty licorice

Roald loved licorice strings, but one of his friends told him a disgusting story. He said that the licorice was made from boiled and squashed rats. Roald did not stop eating licorice strings, but he did start to think of ways to make surprising sweets.

The Llandaff Cathedral in Cardiff, Wales, is close to where Roald lived with his family. He went to Llandaff Cathedral School for two years.

Trouble in the candy store

Roald and his friends usually spent their allowance on candy. Roald especially liked the massive jawbreakers that changed color as you sucked them.

The only problem with his local candy store was the woman who owned it. Mrs. Pratchett did not seem to like little boys. Can you think of some characters like her in Roald Dahl's books? (Try looking in *Matilda* or *The Witches*.)

A dirty trick

It was not long before Roald and his friends took revenge on Mrs. Pratchett. They decided to hide a dead mouse in the jawbreaker jar, which gave her a huge shock. Roald played practical jokes like this throughout his life. Many of his characters are fond of playing tricks, too.

Boarding school

At the age of nine, Roald was sent away to a boys' **boarding school**. He was very homesick, but he did not complain. At that time, school principals would punish students by beating them with a cane, and the principal of Roald's school was very strict. The school also had a cruel **matron** (a woman who was supposed to take care of the students).

Only one adult was kind to the boys. Mrs. O'Connor read them exciting stories every Saturday. She encouraged Roald to read a wide range of books.

Miss Honey and Miss Trunchbull

In the story *Matilda*, there are two different teachers: kind Miss Honey and horrible Miss Trunchbull. Some people think that Roald based these characters on real adults at his boarding school. Miss Honey is like Mrs. O'Connor. Miss Trunchbull is like the frightening school matron.

This is Miss Trunchbull from the movie *Matilda*. Miss Trunchbull is mean and does not like children.

Roald at Repton

The last school Roald attended was a famous boarding school called Repton. The principal of this school was also strict, but Roald enjoyed some parts of school life. He was good at sports and photography.

Roald and the chocolate factory

For Roald, the best thing about Repton School was the chocolate factory that was nearby. The factory owners asked the students at the school to try out their new chocolate bars. Roald remembered this experience when he wrote *Charlie and the Chocolate Factory*.

When he was 13, Roald went to Repton School. He liked playing sports.

Charlie and the Chocolate Factory

Charlie and the Chocolate Factory tells the story of Charlie and four other children who each find a golden ticket that allows them to visit a chocolate factory. Willy Wonka takes them on a tour. They see tiny people, known as the Oompa-Loompas, busy making candy.

Special candy

Willy Wonka's factory produces some truly extraordinary candy. There are everlasting jawbreakers, marshmallow pillows, lickable wallpaper, and many more. Just imagine how fun it would be to try Willy Wonka's inventions!

Candy-tasting

In this **mime** activity, you can pretend to taste some of Willy Wonka's inventions. Then you can show how they make you feel. Ask a friend to guess what kind of candy you are eating and to say what is happening to you.

As you start to eat, think about which **facial expressions** you will make. Will you smile, frown, or look surprised? Then think of what you will do as the candy takes effect. How will you move your arms and legs?

Steps to follow:

1. Pretend you are eating Willy Wonka's Chewing-Gum Meal, a three-course meal in a single stick of gum. First, you taste slurpy tomato soup. Then you taste chewy roast beef and a baked potato. Last comes the sweet, gooey taste of blueberry pie.

2. Now try eating Hair Toffee. It comes in long, sticky strings, and as you begin to chew it, you feel an itchy tingling on your head and chin. Long hair starts to grow!

3. Imagine you are drinking a Fizzy Lifting Drink. As it pops and crackles in your mouth, you feel lighter and lighter, until you start to float above the ground!

Adult Adventures

After Roald left school, he went to work for an oil company in Africa. He was impressed by all the wild animals he saw. Later, he put many African animals into his stories and poems.

Flying high

Soon after World War II began, Roald joined the British Royal Air Force. He trained as a pilot. After one year of flying, he crashed his plane. He went blind for a few weeks and had to have his nose rebuilt. In spite of the danger, Roald loved the excitement of flying. He later wrote scenes about flying in *James and the Giant Peach* and *Charlie and the Great Glass Elevator*.

The Enormous Crocodile is set in Africa and stars a crocodile, monkey, elephant, and hippo.

Roald in the United States

After three years of flying, Roald was sent to the United States, where he worked for the British government. While he was living there, he began to write stories. During the next 18 years, he wrote many stories for adults. Like his children's books, the stories were often gruesome, with exciting **plots** and a lot of surprises.

Roald Dahl loved skyscrapers. *James and the Giant Peach* ends with the peach stuck on the spike of the Empire State Building in New York City!

This photograph shows Roald Dahl with his first wife, Patricia, and three of their five children—Olivia, Tessa, and Theo.

Family life

While he was living in New York, Roald married a U.S. actress named Patricia Neal. They were married for 30 years and had 5 children.

As his children grew older, Roald began to make up stories for them. In 1961 he published his first children's book, *James and the Giant Peach*. For the rest of his life, Roald concentrated on writing for children.

Moving to the country

Roald missed his homeland, and in around 1960 he decided to move back to the United Kingdom. The Dahl family moved to an old farmhouse in the village of Great Missenden, in southern England. Gipsy House had a beautiful garden and was surrounded by fields and woods.

Country stories

Roald loved the country, but he hated hunting and cruelty to animals. *The Magic Finger* and *Danny the Champion of the World* both tell stories about tricks played on hunters.

Sad times

The children in the Dahl family had some terrible tragedies. When Theo Dahl was four months old, his stroller was hit by a taxicab, and he was seriously injured. The next year, seven-year-old Olivia died from measles. Roald **dedicated** *The BFG* to her.

The Roald Dahl Museum and Story Center is located in the village where Roald Dahl lived for 30 years.

A Lifetime of Writing

Roald kept writing until the end of his life. He died at the age of 74. He had a special hut in his backyard where he went to write and think on his own. He tried to spend four hours a day in his writing hut.

Short stories for children

Many people know about Dahl's books, but he also wrote several short stories for children. *Fantastic Mr. Fox* describes how a smart fox tricks three stupid farmers. In *The Twits* some mischievous animals play practical jokes on the revolting Mr. and Mrs. Twit. *Esio Trot* tells the story of a tortoise and some magic spells. (Try saying Esio Trot backward!)

This photograph shows Roald in his writing hut. He wrote as he sat in a comfortable old chair.

This is a scene from the James Bond movie *You Only Live Twice*. Roald Dahl loved the excitement of the James Bond stories, and in 1996 he joined the team working on this movie.

Funny poems

Roald wrote three books of poetry. *Dirty Beasts* is a collection of poems about animals. *Revolting Rhymes* and *Rhyme Stew* both include some strange versions of fairy tales. Just like Roald's stories, his poems can make you giggle and squirm!

Movie scripts

Did you know that Roald Dahl wrote the **screenplay** for the James Bond movie *You Only Live Twice*? He also wrote part of the script for the children's movie *Chitty Chitty Bang Bang*. (You can find out more about movie writing in the *Writing a Screenplay* book in this series.)

Words and pictures

All of Roald Dahl's children's books have illustrations, and most of them were drawn by Quentin Blake. The two men worked very closely together. Quentin Blake was one of the few people who was allowed inside Roald's writing hut.

Quentin Blake's style is easy to recognize. He draws in ink, using lots of scribbly lines to create a sense of movement and excitement. Sometimes he uses watercolor paints to add color to his drawings.

Roald Dahl and Quentin Blake had a lot of fun working together.

Picture it yourself

Looking at pictures helps to bring a book to life, but you can also imagine the scenes in your head. Everyone has their own idea of how Roald Dahl's characters should look.

Steps to follow:

1. Listen to one of Roald's poems or stories being read aloud.

2. Now draw what you see in your head. It could be a character or a whole scene. Ask your friends to draw a picture, too.

3. Compare your picture with the ones your friends have drawn. Do the pictures look exactly the same?

Now try writing a poem or a short story of your own, and draw a picture to illustrate it.

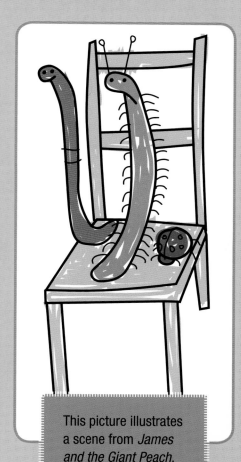

This picture illustrates a scene from *James and the Giant Peach*. Use your own ideas to draw a scene from a Roald Dahl book.

This is an illustration for a made-up story.

A Very Special Writer

Roald Dahl's stories reflect his love for adventure and his sense of mischief. When he was asked what made his books so special, he replied, "I only write about things that are exciting or funny. Children know I'm on their side."

Magic and surprises

Some people think that Roald's stories are like modern fairy tales. They describe battles between good and bad characters, and they often involve some kind of magic. Some of them even have fairy-tale characters such as giants, witches, and animals that talk.

The element of magic helps to create a very exciting story. Magic is also found in the story *Alice in Wonderland* and in the adventures of Harry Potter. Are there other books that remind you of Roald Dahl's stories?

Roald Dahl's stories are easy to read—and they can make you laugh out loud.

Making jokes

In 2008 a prize was set up in memory of Roald Dahl. The Roald Dahl Funny Prize is awarded to the funniest children's books every year. The prize is a great way to remember a writer whose books are full of fun and jokes.

This is a scene from the play *The Witches*. Roald's stories make very exciting plays.

Timeline

1916	Roald Dahl is born in Cardiff, Wales.
1918	World War I ends.
1920	Astri Dahl dies from untreated **appendicitis**. Two months later Roald's father, Harald, dies from **pneumonia**.
1923	Roald leaves his first school, Elmtree House, and goes to Llandaff Cathedral School.
1925	Roald goes to St. Peter's School.
1929	Roald goes to Repton School.
1934	Roald leaves Repton School and starts to work in London for the Shell Oil Company.
1938	Shell sends Roald to work in Tanzania in Africa.
1939	World War II begins. Roald joins the British Royal Air Force and starts training as a pilot.
1940	Roald crashes his plane.
1942	Roald is sent to Washington, D.C., to work for the British government. He starts writing for adults.
1945	World War II ends.
1953	Roald marries Patricia Neal, a U.S. movie star.
1955	Olivia Dahl is born.
1957	Tessa Dahl is born.
1960	Theo Dahl is born. When he is four months old, his stroller is hit by a taxicab.

1961	*James and the Giant Peach* is published.
1962	Olivia Dahl dies from a serious case of measles.
1963	A **vaccine** to protect against measles becomes available.
1964	Ophelia Dahl is born. *Charlie and the Chocolate Factory* is published.
1965	Lucy Dahl is born. While Roald's wife was pregnant, she had three strokes. Roald works very hard to help his wife recover.
1966	Roald writes the **screenplay** for the James Bond movie *You Only Live Twice*.
1975	*Danny the Champion of the World* is published.
1981	*George's Marvellous Medicine* is published.
1982	*The BFG* is published.
1983	Roald and Patricia are divorced. Roald marries Felicity Crosland. *The Witches* is published.
1988	*Matilda* is published.
1990	Roald dies at the age of 74.

Glossary

appendicitis pain and high temperature caused by an infected appendix (a small, closed tube in the stomach). People can die from appendicitis if their appendix is not removed quickly.

boarding school school where students live. They sleep and eat there.

dedicated made or written for someone as a special gift. Roald dedicated *The BFG* to his daughter Olivia, who died in 1962.

facial expression movement made by your face to show feelings and emotions. Smiling and frowning are both facial expressions.

matron woman who works at a school. Her job is to take care of the students if they get sick.

mime act using movements and actions instead of words

plot story of a book, movie, or play. Whatever he wrote, Roald's plots were always exciting and surprising.

pneumonia serious lung disease that makes breathing difficult. Roald's father died from pneumonia.

screenplay written version of the words and actions in a movie. A script is a different word for a screenplay.

vaccine something that is given in an injection in order to prevent people from getting a disease

Find Out More

Books

Hook, Jason. *Roald Dahl: The Storyteller* (*Famous Lives*). Chicago: Raintree, 2004.

Ruffin, Frances E. *Meet Roald Dahl* (*About the Author*). New York: PowerKids, 2006.

Woog, Adam. *Roald Dahl* (*Inventors and Creators*). Detroit: KidHaven, 2005.

Here is a list of some of Roald Dahl's books, and when they were first published.
Charlie and the Chocolate Factory (1964)
Danny the Champion of the World (1975)
James and the Giant Peach (1961)
Matilda (1988)
The BFG (1982)
The Twits (1980)
The Witches (1983)

Websites

www.roalddahl.com
The official website of Roald Dahl contains lots of information about the author's life and books.

Index

adenoids 9
African animals 18
Alice in Wonderland 26
Amundsen, Roald 6

BFG, The 4, 5, 10, 11, 21
Blake, Quentin 24
boarding school 14, 15
Boy: Tales of Childhood 6, 9
British Royal Air Force 18

candy-tasting 17
candy and chocolate 12–13, 15, 16–17
characters 10, 13, 14, 25, 26, 27
Charlie and the Chocolate Factory 4, 5, 15, 16
Charlie and the Great Glass Elevator 18
Chitty Chitty Bang Bang 23

Dahl, Olivia 20, 21
Dahl, Roald
  Africa, work in 18
  air force pilot 18, 19
  country, love of the 20
  death 22
  early life 6–15
  family background 7, 8
  imagination 4
  marriage and children 20–21
  poetry 4, 23
  school days 12, 14–15
  screenplays 23
  short stories 22
  United States, working in 19

Dahl, Tessa 20
Dahl, Theo 20, 21
dance 11
Danny the Champion of the World 4, 20
Dirty Beasts 23

Empire State Building 19
Enormous Crocodile, The 18
Esio Trot 22

facial expressions 17
fairy tales 9, 23, 26
Fantastic Mr. Fox 22

George's Marvellous Medicine 6
giants 8, 10, 11, 26
The Giraffe and the Pelly and Me 5
Great Missenden 20, 21
gruesome stories 9, 19

Harry Potter adventures 26

illustrations 24, 25

James and the Giant Peach 4, 18, 19, 20, 25
jawbreakers 13

licorice 12
Llandaff Cathedral School 12

magic 26
Magic Finger, The 20
Matilda 4, 13, 14
mime 17
music 11

Neal, Patricia 20
New York City 19, 20
Norway 7, 8, 9

plots 19
poetry 4, 23
practical jokes 13
Pratchett, Mrs. 13

Repton School 15
Revolting Rhymes 23
Rhyme Stew 23
Roald Dahl Funny Prize 27
Roald Dahl Museum and Story Center 21, 22

school matron 14
screenplays 23
short stories 22
South Pole 6

teachers 14
Twits, The 9, 22

United States 19, 20

Wales 7, 12
witches 8, 9, 27
Witches, The 9, 13, 27
Wonka, Willy 5, 16, 17
words, surprising 5, 27
World War II 18
writing hut 22, 24

You Only Live Twice 23